THE DRIVING BOOK FOR TEENS

The DRIVING BOOK for TEENS

A Beginner's Guide to Becoming a Safe, Smart, and Skilled Driver

MAUREEN STILES

ROCKRIDGE
PRESS

**To Mark, Mac, Drew, and Reed for your
patience as I squirreled away writing.
My gratitude and love are deep and eternal.**

Contents

How to Use This Book

Welcome to *The Driving Book for Teens!* This book is a general guide and resource for teenagers who want to earn their license, as well as newly licensed drivers. It offers an overview of the rules of the road, helpful test preparation, important safety tips, and essential things to know about cars and car maintenance.

I have spent hundreds of hours teaching my three kids to drive. They have all grown into responsible drivers who treat driving as a privilege. This book combines my observations and experience teaching driving over the last decade.

With this book, you'll get strategies and tools to improve your driving, no matter your skill level. Please note that this book is not meant to replace any formal driver's education required in your state. If you are under eighteen years old, you still need permission to drive from your parent or guardian. Here's what the book will cover:

Chapter 1 explains road rules, like using signals, passing cars, and sharing the road. These rules apply in most of the United States, but be sure to read your state's Motor Vehicle Services manual to check specifics. Your driver's education materials will also be a good resource.

Chapters 2 and 3 cover how to prepare for the written test and the driving test. Try answering the sample questions and go over the tips for taking the road test. Check your answers against the Answer Key to test your knowledge. Go back to the questions you got wrong and try again. Practicing will help you feel more confident on test day.

Chapter 4 covers the basics of a typical dashboard and how to take care of a car. Because every car is different, it is your responsibility to read the owner's manual of your car. You can come back to this chapter whenever you run into issues or have questions about your car.

Chapters 5 and 6 give you practical advice for the road. They cover some common situations you may encounter when driving. You'll learn how to deal with distractions, different types of roads, and emergencies. You will also get checklists to use before heading to your destination, plus what to do before you exit the car.

Driving gives you freedom and possibilities, but it also comes with great responsibility. Respect the road and its rules, and driving can become one of the great pleasures of your life.

Good luck and safe driving!

Part 1

RULES, TEST PREP, AND PRACTICE

CHAPTER 1

Rules of the Road

F ollowing the rules of the road is important. Not only is it a courtesy to other drivers, but it also saves lives. Defensive driving is an important part of safe driving. Driving defensively means staying alert so you can respond when other drivers don't follow the rules. Come back to this chapter whenever you need a reminder about universal road rules. Note that some rules vary from place to place, so you will need to research laws specific to your state, like speed limits.

Road Signs, Lines, and Signals

Road rules might look overwhelming, and you don't have to memorize all of them right now. But once you read, practice, and gain experience, these rules will become automatic. The following rules of the road apply everywhere in the United States:

 RED LIGHT: Come to a complete stop at the intersection, even if you're turning right afterward.

 YELLOW LIGHT: Slow down and attempt to stop completely by the time the light turns red.

 GREEN LIGHT: Keep driving at the same speed through the light but watch for turning cars and pedestrians.

 STOP SIGN: Come to a full stop at the stop sign. Then, look in all directions and proceed when it is safe.

 YIELD SIGN: Usually an upside-down triangle, this sign means you must let cars already on the road go first as you enter the roadway.

 RAILROAD CROSSING SIGN: A railroad crossing is ahead. Be prepared to stop when you see any sign with the word "Railroad" on it.

ONE-WAY SIGN: Where this sign is posted, traffic goes in only one direction; no two-way traffic is allowed.

 SPEED LIMIT SIGNS: These indicate the maximum safe speed under ideal conditions. If there is rain, ice, etc., on the road, the safe driving speed may be lower.

 BLUE SIGNS: These signs provide information about upcoming gas stations, hotels, restaurants, and rest areas.

 BROWN SIGNS: These signs provide information about upcoming parks and recreation services.

 ORANGE SIGNS: These signs alert you to upcoming construction.

 GREEN HORIZONTAL SIGNS: These signs provide information on upcoming routes, highway exits, and miles to upcoming cities and towns.

 DIAMOND-SHAPED SIGNS: Be ready for nearby driving obstacles (divided highway, sharp curve, etc.).

 PENTAGON-SHAPED SIGNS: Take caution because there is a school or pedestrian crossing nearby.

 SHIELD-SHAPED SIGNS: These signs let you know you are traveling on a US route.

 BLUE SIGN MARKED WITH AN "H": You are approaching an exit or route to a hospital.

YELLOW LINES ON ROAD: These lines dictate when you can or cannot pass other cars when driving. They can be solid or dotted. See Passing on page 10 for more information.

LANE MARKINGS: An "X" above a lane on a multilane road means that lane is closed to traffic.

RED PAINTED CURB: This means you can't stop, stand, or park along this curb.

BLUE PAINTED PARKING SPACE: This means a parking space is reserved for drivers with disabilities, who have an appropriate placard.

Speed

According to the Centers for Disease Control (CDC), excessive speed is a leading cause of accidents among teen drivers. The faster you travel, the harder it is for you to react to sudden changes and control your car. Speed limits are based on road configuration and traffic flow studies.

SPEED LIMITS: These are the maximum speeds you can drive under ideal circumstances (no snow, rain, or ice). Look for the speed limit each time you are on a new road.

SPEEDOMETER: You are responsible for monitoring your speed using the car's speedometer to make sure you are driving under the speed limit.

MINIMUM SPEEDS: It is also not safe to drive significantly under the speed limit. Avoid driving too slowly unless it is necessary for safety reasons.

NO POSTED SPEEDS: It is important to know the speed rules of your state if there are no posted speed signs in a suburb or neighborhood.

TRAFFIC FLOW: Keeping up with the flow of traffic is not an excuse to exceed the speed limit.

BAD WEATHER: Reduce speed as soon as the pavement gets wet.

SLOW LANE: Slower drivers should stay in the right lane on highways.

OBSTACLES: Always reduce speed when traveling over a speed bump or when on unpaved roads.

Safe Following and Stopping Distance

Leaving space between your car and the one in front of you helps avoid collisions. To follow other cars safely, you must know your car's stopping distance. Stopping distance is how long it takes for your car to come to a stop in an emergency.

Stopping distance is like an algebra problem: Your car is the constant and the variable is your speed. Your car will need different spacing depending on how fast it's moving. The faster your car travels, the more time it takes to stop. That means you must always be calculating stopping distances as you drive at different speeds to follow at a safe distance.

THREE-SECOND RULE: This is the recommended space between cars. To calculate how much space to leave, watch the car ahead of you pass an object on the side of the road, like a road sign. Then count how many seconds it takes for you to get to the same object. You should arrive at that object three seconds later. If you reach the object in less than three seconds, you are driving too close to the car in front of you.

BAD WEATHER: In bad weather, increase the following distance between you and the car in front of you. This is because it takes longer to stop a car in rain, snow, or sleet.

THE CAR BEHIND YOU: If other cars are not practicing safe distance, move over and let them pass.

WEIGHT: Heavier vehicles take longer to stop. If you are carrying a heavy load for vacation, moving, or even extra passengers, take that into consideration when calculating stopping distance.

Turns

Turns require navigating not only your current road, but also the road you are turning onto. This is more complicated than it looks. But with focus and awareness, you can make turns safely! Practice turns in a large, empty parking lot to determine the necessary space to turn your vehicle without hitting a curb or oncoming traffic. This is known as the turn radius. Here are some rules to keep in mind:

SIGNALING: Always use turn signals even in designated turn lanes.

MULTIPLE TURN LANES: Larger roads may have multiple lanes for turning in the same direction. Always end your turn in the same lane in which you started.

PEDESTRIANS: Always yield to pedestrians, even if they are walking against a light or signal.

RIGHT ON RED: Turn only after coming to a full stop, checking for pedestrians and cars turning left in front of you.

WHEN NOT TO TURN RIGHT ON RED: Right turn on red is not allowed in all states or at all intersections. Know your state laws and look for signs before turning right on red.

U-TURNS: A U-turn is just like it sounds. It's turning in a "U" shape to change direction. Look for signs prohibiting U-turns. If you're not comfortable making a U-turn, simply go around the block to change direction. Remember, you can never cross a double yellow line to make a U-turn.

Passing

You can think of passing cars as a privilege. It can be a useful driving tool but only under the right circumstances.

SOLID YELLOW LINE: On a two-way road, a solid yellow line means no passing permitted. Don't cross this line.

BROKEN/DOTTED YELLOW OR WHITE LINE: On a two-way road, a broken yellow or white line means you can cross this line to pass cars when it's safe to do so.

NO PASSING ON TWO-WAY ROADS: There is no passing allowed on hills or 100 feet before a tunnel or bridge. Never pass cars to the right of the road or on the shoulder.

PREPARING TO PASS: Scan the horizon for oncoming traffic and check side and rearview mirrors for other drivers attempting to pass. Move within two seconds' stopping distance of the car you are trying to pass.

PASSING: Turn on the left signal, check for oncoming traffic and mirrors again, move into the left lane, and accelerate within the speed limit until the car you are trying to pass is behind you and visible in the rearview mirror.

RETURNING TO LANE: Turn on the right signal, check that the car you just passed is still behind you, and move right into the original lane.

LETTING OTHERS PASS: If a car wants to pass you, maintain speed and allow the car room to pass and merge in front of you.

MULTIPLE LANE ROADS: The left lane is solely for passing slower cars. See more on highway passing in chapter 6 (page 103).

NO PASSING: Never pass another car to beat a railroad signal or a yellow light, or to avoid a car stopped for pedestrians.

Intersections

When roads cross, they form an intersection. At intersections, vehicles coming from different directions are occupying the same space at the same time. Drivers must yield to one another and follow posted signals and signs. Here are some basic rules to follow at intersections:

CROSSWALKS: Most intersections are marked with crosswalks or stop lines on the road marking where pedestrians can cross. Your front bumper should not cross these lines.

APPROACH: As you approach an intersection, make sure you are in the proper lane, whether you are going straight or turning. Before proceeding, look left, then right, and left again to check for traffic and pedestrians, even if you have the right-of-way.

GREEN LIGHT: After your light turns green, count to two and then proceed if the intersection is clear of cross traffic.

RED LIGHT: Remain stopped without inching forward in anticipation of the green light.

YELLOW LIGHT: Slow down and prepare to stop as soon you see a yellow light. It is dangerous to speed up and race through the intersection.

FOUR-WAY STOP: When drivers arrive at the same time and there are no traffic lights, drivers yield to the car to the right of them.

SIGNALING: Use turn signals at intersections so other drivers know your intentions.

STAGGERED STOPS: In some streets, stop lines are set back from the intersection to make room for larger vehicles or narrow roads needing a wide turn radius.

ROUNDABOUTS: Roundabouts, also known as traffic circles, are lanes that move counterclockwise around an island in the middle. Exiting is always to the right.

Sharing the Road

Part of good driving is being a good citizen. Share the road with other vehicles—large and small. Look out for pedestrians and remember that they always have the right-of-way.

BICYCLES: Even without a bike lane, bicycle riders have the right to share the road. If you want to pass a bicycle, slow down, allow extra stopping distance, and wait until it is safe.

MOTORCYCLES: Motorcycles are smaller than cars and harder to see. Follow the rules of the road regarding signals, and check blind spots and mirrors often to keep motorcyclists and yourself safe. Motorcycles lack the self-canceling turn signals many cars have. Do not assume a motorcycle is turning just because its signal is blinking. Wait until the motorcycle passes to change lanes or enter the roadway.

PEDESTRIANS: Pedestrians always have the right-of-way even if they are walking against a light or crosswalk.

TRUCKS: Driving on any highway means you're sharing the road with large trucks. Due to their weight, large trucks need extra stopping time. Never change lanes quickly in front of a truck. Also be aware of blind spots (see more in chapter 6, page 88) and maneuvering challenges that trucks face.

ANIMALS: Growth of infrastructure has pushed more animals closer to roads and highways. See more about watching for animals in chapter 6, page 92.

Yielding to Other Vehicles

In certain situations, drivers must follow specific rules regarding other vehicles on the road. Here are some things you may encounter:

EMERGENCY VEHICLES

- Emergency vehicles always have the right-of-way. If a vehicle is behind you with sirens and lights on, pull over to one side to allow them to pass. Once the emergency vehicle has passed, check your mirrors and wait until there is space to safely reenter the roadway.

- You can proceed through a red light if it is the only way to let an emergency vehicle pass. Check oncoming traffic or use your horn as a warning to cross traffic if applicable.

SCHOOL BUSES

- School buses have flashing lights and a stop sign to alert drivers when dropping off or picking up schoolchildren. All drivers behind the school bus or coming from the opposite direction, and there is not a median in the road, must stop completely until the lights are turned off and the stop sign is withdrawn.

- Drivers traveling in the opposite direction and separated from a school bus by a raised or grassy median may proceed with caution even if the bus is stopped and the lights are flashing.

- School buses must come to a full stop at a railroad track even if there is no train or alert.

TRAINS

- Trains cannot swerve or stop quickly, so drivers are responsible for avoiding trains and obeying railroad crossing signals. That means you must watch and listen for trains and alarm bells before attempting to cross any railroad tracks.

Headlights

Headlights not only illuminate a car's path, but they also announce your location to other drivers. Headlights should be on from sunset to sunrise. Be sure to learn the laws in your own state. Here are tips for how to use and maintain headlights properly:

BAD WEATHER

- Turn on headlights any time you are using windshield wipers, even in the daytime.

- In fog, slow your speed and keep headlights on low. Do not use high beams.

HIGH BEAMS

- When using high beams on a rural road with low light, switch back to low beams if a car is approaching.

- If a car is in front of you, do not use high beams; it blocks rear vision for that driver.

- If an approaching car is using high beams, shift your eyes to the right outer edge of your lane until the car passes.

MAINTENANCE

- You can receive a fine for not using headlights when required or for having broken headlights.

- Look at the reflection of your headlights on the bumpers of other cars and the road. They should be aligned and straight. If not, they need adjustment.

- Make sure to check if your headlights turn on with the engine any time it is dark, or if they manually turn off and on.

- Some vehicles have "running lights" or smaller head lamps that turn on whenever the engine is running.

Parking

How you leave your car idle is just as important as how you maneuver it in motion.

WHERE TO PARK: Look for signs that restrict parking before leaving your parked car. Do not ignore meters or paid parking, as violations can lead to tickets and fines.

BE COURTEOUS: Stay within the parking lines and carefully enter and exit the car if space is tight.

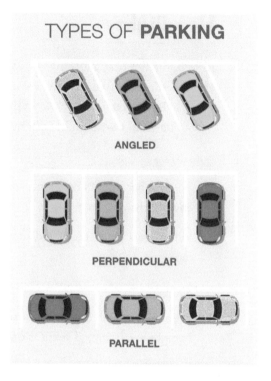

TYPES OF **PARKING**

ANGLED

PERPENDICULAR

PARALLEL

CHECK PARKING: Look at the placement of your car after you park. Is it straight? Is it impeding traffic in any way? If your car is crooked, try again

PARALLEL PARKING: Parallel parking is not on every driving test but is a valuable skill to learn.

EXITING: The driver exiting a parking space is responsible for checking for oncoming traffic, other parked vehicles, or those driving in the lot.

PARKING UPHILL: Parking on an uphill with a curb requires pulling in and turning the wheels away from the curb so it will angle the car back toward the curb if it slides. Parking on an uphill without a curb requires pulling in and turning the wheels away from traffic so the car will drift off the road if it moves.

PARKING DOWNHILL: Parking on a downhill with a curb requires pulling in and turning the wheels toward the curb so it will angle the car back toward the curb if it slides. Parking on a downhill without a curb requires pulling in and turning the wheels away from traffic so the car will drift off the road if it moves.

Safety

The term "safety" covers a lot of ground. It includes everything from car maintenance and following rules of the road, to knowing when you need assistance from a guardian, mechanic, or police officer. As a new driver you need to be extra cautious. Never hesitate to ask experienced drivers for advice. Here are some basic tips that will help keep you safe:

UNOCCUPIED CAR: Never leave an unoccupied car with the engine running, even if it is "just for a minute."

KEYS: Never leave keys in a car, including when parked in a garage or driveway.

CHECK SURROUNDINGS: Always be aware of your surroundings. Pull over in a safe place if you are lost.

DEFENSIVE DRIVING: Always look out for and anticipate errors other drivers might make.

TIME MANAGEMENT: Give yourself plenty of time to arrive at your destination without having to speed or take shortcuts.

SHORTCUTS: It is dangerous to cut through a gas station or parking lot to avoid a light or save time; it is also illegal in many states.

CHAPTER 2

Preparing for the Written Test

There is a reason the written portion of the driving test is hard. After all, a passing grade means you are permitted to drive an actual car on the road with an adult. That is a big step and one that requires serious prep work.

This chapter will help set you up for success with sample questions on universal road rules. Note that some questions in this chapter address driving rules that may be different from state to state. Use the fill-in-the-blank questions to research rules specific to your state.

Tips for Acing Your Written Test

If you are feeling nervous about taking the written driver's test, don't worry. That's completely normal! The only way to feel more comfortable is to practice and study. The practice tests are meant to show you your weaknesses in licensing knowledge. That is just as important as what you have mastered when it comes to driving. Remember that there is no set timeline for testing, permitting, and licensure. Take your time until you feel comfortable and ready to move through each step. Here are some tips for taking the written test:

STATE MANUAL: Download and study your state's Motor Vehicle Services manual.

PRACTICE EXAMS: Take the online practice tests on your state's Motor Vehicle Services website.

ASK QUESTIONS: If confused, ask questions of experienced drivers.

ROOM SETUP: If you can, find someone who has taken the written test recently and ask about the room setup and any obstacles they might have encountered.

TIME MANAGEMENT: Know how much time is allotted to complete the test and what percentage is needed to pass.

DRIVER'S EDUCATION: If you have taken driver's education before the test, study those notes as well.

DRIVING SCHOOL

Enrolling in an accredited driver's education program is required in most states. The laws surrounding driver's education programs vary from state to state and include age requirements and online opportunities. Check your state's Motor Vehicle Services website for more information. Make sure you choose a program that is listed as accepted through your state's Motor Vehicle Services office. Your driver's education program should include in-car instruction to practice skills that will be tested on the road portion of the driver's test. This is in addition to what you may be working on outside of classes with an adult. Many programs have provisions for financial aid and payment options if necessary.

Practice Multiple-Choice Questions

This section has seventy-five multiple-choice questions that you might see on your written test. These are not state specific. You can find the answers in the Answer Key (page 109) as well as in your supplemental driver's education materials.

1. **When is it acceptable to make a right turn on red?**

   a) Always

   b) After stopping to check for obstacles and signage

   c) Never

   d) If a sign is posted authorizing turns

2. **If a car is equipped with airbags, seat belts are used by**

   a) Everyone in the car

   b) Back seat passengers only

   c) Front seat passengers only

   d) Driver only

3. **A flashing yellow light indicates**

   a) Slow down or caution

   b) Merging traffic

   c) Stop and proceed when clear

   d) Keep driving at speed

4. **A flashing red light indicates**

   a) Proceed as if at a stop sign

   b) Proceed as if at a yield sign

   c) Keep driving unless it is solid red

   d) Both b and c

5. **When approaching a construction work zone, you should**

   a) Slow down and follow signs and signals

   b) Expect the unexpected

   c) Expect construction vehicles and workers to yield to cars

   d) Both a and b

6. **When losing traction or hydroplaning (losing traction because water gets between your tires and the road), you should**

   a) Brake hard

   b) Maintain speed

   c) Steer one way or the other to gain control

   d) Shift the car into neutral

7. **When driving in the rain, you should**

   a) Use high beams

   b) Decrease distance between cars

   c) Speed up to get home

   d) Increase distance between cars

8. What is an example of distracted driving?

   a) Traveling with kids and pets as passengers

   b) Eating

   c) Texting when driving

   d) All of the above

9. When is the road most slippery?

   a) After raining for a long time

   b) When rain first begins

   c) When there are big puddles

   d) During a heavy downpour

10. When approaching a railroad crossing, you should

   a) Proceed if you don't hear a train

   b) Speed up to cross the tracks before a train comes

   c) Slow down and cross safely if there are no train or alerts

   d) Come to a complete stop and wait for a train

11. At a four-way stop with other drivers, you should

   a) Go first if you are going straight

   b) Yield to the car on the right

   c) Yield to the car on the left

   d) Go first if you are turning

12. Alcohol and drugs are permitted when driving

a) If you have only a little

b) If you wait an hour before driving

c) Never

d) Always

13. When encountering an emergency vehicle, you should

a) Stop immediately

b) Speed up to get out of the way

c) Pull to the side of the road and wait for it to pass

d) Follow it

14. Pedestrians have the right-of-way

a) Only in crosswalks

b) When obeying traffic signals, signs, and marked crosswalks

c) Never

d) In suburban areas

15. In a traffic circle or roundabout drivers should

a) Exit from the left

b) Yield to cars in the circle

c) Exit to the right

d) Both b and c

16. Disabled parking spaces are

a) For everyone if empty

b) For everyone if parking only for a short time

c) For senior citizens

d) For those with a disability placard on their car

17. Check the gas gauge before leaving

a) When driving long distances

b) Always

c) If the gas light is on

d) Once a week

18. When approaching a curve, you should

a) Speed up

b) Slow down

c) Use the shoulder

d) Both b and c

19. Use turn signals

a) Only if a car is following you

b) Only at intersections

c) Every time you turn

d) Only at night

20. Drivers are responsible for knowing speed limits

a) When first entering a roadway

b) Only in residential areas

c) Only on the highway

d) Always

21. Excessive speed

a) Impairs reaction time

b) Is okay if you know the road

c) Endangers other drivers

d) Both a and c

22. When driving in fog, you should

a) Use high beam headlights

b) Use low beam headlights

c) Put on your hazard lights

d) Both a and c

23. The three-second rule applies to

a) The time allotted to pull over if an emergency vehicle is behind you

b) The time you have before a yellow light turns red

c) The spacing between your car and the one in front of you

d) The time needed to go through an intersection

24. A double yellow line means

a) Passing permitted

b) Trucks cannot pass

c) No passing

d) Right lane may pass after checking oncoming traffic

25. If faced with aggressive driving, you should

a) Challenge the other driver

b) Speed up

c) Honk your horn repeatedly

d) Move out of their way and don't make eye contact

26. If pulled over by a police officer, you should

a) Exit the car immediately and approach the officer

b) Ask as many questions as you can

c) Wait in the car and roll down the window when approached

d) Think of a good story

27. A single broken white center line

a) Is only on roads with traffic flowing in the same direction

b) Means cars may not pass

c) Means cars may pass

d) Both a and c

28. How do you pass a cyclist with no bike lane?

a) Honk your horn at the cyclist until they move

b) Give the cyclist space

c) Slow down and pass only when you have the room to do so safely

d) Both b and c

29. When entering an interstate from an on-ramp, you should

a) Yield to drivers already on the interstate

b) Expect drivers to yield to you

c) Accelerate immediately to match the flow of traffic

d) Honk your horn until someone lets you in

30. An arrow painted on the pavement

a) Means that drivers in that lane must follow the arrow right, left, or straight

b) Means that drivers have the option of following the arrow right, left, or straight

c) Isn't enforceable

d) Is only for emergency vehicles

31. If stopping along the road at night, you should

a) Turn off headlights

b) Use parking lights only

c) Use headlights only

d) Turn on hazard flashers and leave headlights on

32. Seat belts should be adjusted until

a) They fit loosely over the shoulder and lap

b) They fit snugly across the shoulder and lap

c) The seat belt alarm stops chiming

d) They can be fastened behind you

33. When using reverse to back up, you should

a) Use rearview and side mirrors for guidance

b) Use only rearview mirror

c) Check behind car before getting inside it and before moving

d) Both a and c

34. Examples of distracted driving include

a) Staring into space

b) Making consistent eye contact with passengers

c) Watching the car in front of you

d) Both a and b

35. What is a no-zone?

a) A blind spot around a large vehicle

b) A special speed zone

c) A road with restrictions around passing

d) The zone after a work zone

36. Driving below the speed limit is advisable when

a) You don't feel like driving fast

b) Bad weather makes conditions less than ideal

c) On a four-lane road

d) You think you might get stopped by a police officer

37. Allow more stopping space when

a) On an incline

b) At a stop sign

c) At an intersection

d) At a toll plaza

38. If you miss an exit on a highway or interstate, you should

a) Stop and immediately attempt to cross the median

b) Take the next exit and backtrack

c) Start trying to renavigate on your phone

d) Pull over on the shoulder and reverse until you reach the exit

39. Fully loaded tractor trailers traveling 55 mph will need

a) Less time than a car to come to a stop

b) To travel only in the right lane

c) The same amount of time as a car to come to a stop

d) More time than a car to come to a stop

40. If involved in a minor accident, you should

    a)   Stop immediately and don't move

    b)   Move your vehicle just off the road if possible

    c)   Get insurance information from any other drivers

    d)   Both b and c

41. Motorcycles have

    a)   A right to their own lane

    b)   The same road rules as passenger vehicles

    c)   Blinkers that don't deactivate after a turn

    d)   All of the above

42. In a skid, you should

    a)   Turn the wheel in the direction of the skid

    b)   Turn the wheel in the opposite direction of the skid

    c)   Turn the wheel in any direction

    d)   Keep the steering wheel as straight as you can

43. If you feel tired when driving, you should

    a)   Get a coffee

    b)   Open the window

    c)   Stop driving and pull over in a safe area to rest

    d)   Turn up the radio

44. If a driver behind you repeatedly flashes their headlights, you should

a) Move over and let the car pass

b) Speed up

c) Honk your horn

d) Call the police

45. On a roadway with several lanes in your direction, what lanes are used for passing?

a) All lanes

b) Middle and left lanes

c) Right lanes

d) No lanes

46. The connection of a freeway to a road or another freeway by a series of ramps is _____

a) An entrance ramp

b) An exit ramp

c) A deceleration lane

d) An interchange

47. At intersections, you should follow the

a) Left-right rule

b) Left-right-left rule

c) Right-left-right rule

d) Right-left rule

48. When entering a freeway, your speed should

a) Slowly increase as you move along the on-ramp

b) Accelerate rapidly to catch up

c) Stay below the speed limit until you merge

d) Never go above 30 mph

49. If you are going straight at a stop sign and the vehicle on your left has a right turn signal on, you should

a) Press the gas pedal quickly

b) Honk your horn

c) Make your turn because a signal always means a car is turning

d) Wait until the car begins a turn, then proceed

50. If the road is not wide enough for a U-turn, you should

a) Put the car in reverse

b) Make a four-point turn

c) Make a three-point turn

d) Drive over the curb

51. If a worker directs you with a flag in a work zone, you should

a) Ignore it and follow posted signs

b) Follow all directives

c) Stop and ask questions

d) Call the police

52. To drive safely at night, you should

   a) Increase following distance

   b) Not drive when feeling tired

   c) Make sure headlights are in working order

   d) All of the above

53. When preparing to make a left turn, you should

   a) Gradually slow down and check the rearview mirror

   b) Watch for oncoming cars and pedestrians

   c) Move into the left lane when clear

   d) All of the above

54. If your car becomes stranded in the snow, you should

   a) Leave the car and go for help

   b) Take a nap in the backseat

   c) Stay outside the car and flag down help

   d) Stay in the car and wait for a passerby

55. When driving in icy or snowy conditions, what can you do to avoid a crash?

   a) Add weight to the car to prevent skids

   b) Exit the highway as quickly as possible

   c) Slow down and increase following distance

   d) Use four-wheel drive if you have it

The next set of questions will reference road signs that drivers encounter across the United States.

56. This sign means

a) Do Not Enter during rush hour

b) Do Not Enter at any time

c) Do Not Enter except trucks

d) Do Not Enter before coming to a complete stop first

57. This sign means

a) Pedestrians crossing

b) Stop

c) Slow or stop and yield to other drivers who have the right-of-way

d) You have the right-of-way so other drivers must slow or stop

58. This sign means

a) Right turns on red light permitted

b) No right turns on red light permitted

c) No right turns permitted

d) Right turns from right lane only

59. This sign means

a) Objects in the road

b) Divided roadway

c) One-way roadway

d) Turn right at the next intersection

60. This sign means

a) Stop and proceed when clear

b) Cars on the left stop and proceed when clear

c) Cars on the right stop and proceed when clear

d) Other cars must stop and wait for you to go

61. This sign means

a) Move to the right of the roadway

b) Traffic moves one way to the right

c) Traffic moves one way to the left

d) Only one passenger per car

62. This sign means

a) U-turns permitted after stopping

b) U-turns not permitted

c) U-turns permitted during rush hour

d) U-turns required

63. This sign means

a) Speed limit if it is daytime

b) Speed limit with no traffic

c) Speed limit under optimal road conditions

d) Speed minimum

64. This sign means

a) Family area

b) School crossing

c) Pedestrian crossing

d) Walk in groups for safety

65. This sign means

a) Walk single file

b) School crossing

c) Pedestrian crossing

d) No cars allowed

66. This sign means

a) Santa crossing

b) Deer crossing

c) Animal feeding area

d) Hunting allowed

67. This sign means

a) Railroad station ahead

b) Railroad track crossing ahead

c) No trains crossing

d) Crossing railroad tracks not permitted

68. This sign means

   a) Lanes shift ahead

   b) Winding road ahead

   c) Construction ahead

   d) Bumpy road ahead

69. This sign means

   a) You are on a marked US route

   b) You are in the United States

   c) US road rules apply

   d) You are leaving the United States

70. This sign means

   a) Look to your left

   b) Sharp curve to the left ahead

   c) Left turn ahead

   d) Parking area ahead

71. This sign means

   a) Helipad ahead

   b) Hospital ahead

   c) Hotel ahead

   d) Hazardous road conditions ahead

72. Blue horizontal road signs mean

a) Park and recreation amenities ahead

b) Food, gas, and rest stops ahead

c) Body of water ahead

d) Police station ahead

73. Brown horizontal road signs mean

a) Park and recreation facilities ahead

b) Wooded area ahead

c) Rest stops ahead

d) Full-service gas station ahead

74. Green horizontal road signs mean

a) Picnic area ahead

b) Route, city, and mileage information

c) Proceed straight without stopping

d) Thick forest area ahead

75. Orange signs mean

a) Construction or maintenance ahead

b) Slower speeds ahead

c) Restrooms ahead

d) Foggy area ahead

Fill-in-the-Blank Questions for Your State

Get a copy of your state's Motor Vehicle Services guide because the next set of questions will depend on your state laws and regulations. You need to know both the universal rules of the road as well as specific laws for your state to become a responsible, experienced driver. These questions also cover the process of obtaining your license. You can find the answers to these questions in your state Motor Vehicle Services guide; they are not included in this book's answer key.

1. **Have you read your state's graduated driver licensing (GDL) laws?**

_____

_____

2. **If you answered yes to the previous question, are there restricted driving hours? If you answered no, research the GDL laws and return to this question.**

_____

_____

3. **What are the consequences of a driving violation during the GDL process?**

_____

_____

4. Are you required to take driver's education before the written test, or is it acceptable after you get your permit?

_____

_____

5. What percentage of correct answers is necessary to pass the written portion of the driver's test in your state?

_____

_____

6. What are your state laws regarding handheld phone use?

_____

_____

7. What turns and skills will you be tested on during the road test?

_____

_____

8. Does your state have headlight laws?

_____

_____

9. What speed is considered reckless driving in your state?

_____

_____

10. Does your state have windshield wiper laws? If yes, what are they?

_____

_____

11. What are the fees for obtaining a driver's license in your state?

_____

_____

12. Does your state have "move over" laws?

_____

_____

13. What are the child passenger laws in your state?

_____

_____

14. Does your state have laws regarding passengers for new drivers?

_____

_____

15. When does a provisional license turn to full licensure in your state?

_____

_____

16. Does your state allow tinted windows?

_____

_____

17. What is the maximum speed limit in your state?

_____

_____

18. How often does your state require emissions testing?

_____

_____

19. Is an inspection part of the vehicle registration process in your state?

_____

_____

20. What are the seat belt laws in your state?

_____

_____

21. Does your state have implied speed limits in residential areas if none are posted?

_____

_____

22. Does your state have laws prohibiting exhaust modifications?

_____

_____

23. Does your state use red light and speed cameras?

_____

_____

24. If so, what are the penalties involved?

_____

_____

25. Are there minimum insurance requirements in your state?

_____

_____

26. Are backup cameras and in-car driving aids allowed during the road test in your state?

_____

_____

27. If not, what steps do you need to take for testing if your car has backup camera or other in-car driving aids?

_____

_____

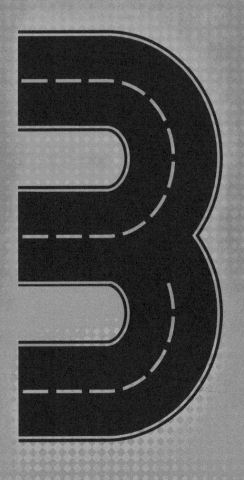

CHAPTER 3

Preparing for the Road Test

I t may seem like the only thing standing between you and the open road is the dreaded road test. But with everything you've learned so far, you are closer than you think! This chapter is your one-stop resource for general information and tips designed for road test success. You'll get an overview of the test itself, plus tips for passing it. Although I aim to make this as comprehensive as possible, it covers only universal rules of the road test across the United States. You are responsible for researching and preparing for state-specific parts of the test.

What to Expect on Test Day

The road test has many moving parts. For example, paperwork verification and mechanical checks are necessary before you can move on to the road test. Knowing as much as you can in advance will help calm nerves as the day approaches. After all, preparation builds confidence! Here are some things to be aware of:

LOGISTICS

- Each state has Motor Vehicle Services offices where tests are conducted. You can test anywhere in your state. Go to your state's Motor Vehicle Services website to find the office nearest you.

- You need a testing appointment in advance.

- There are fees due the day of the driving test, so research in advance the fees and what forms of payment the Motor Vehicle Services accepts.

- Bring your permit, driver's education paperwork, appointment confirmation, and information regarding any graduated licensing requirements.

- Look up directions to the testing location to avoid being late to your road test.

- An adult driver must drive you to the test site and remain until you finish.

TESTING

- The test will most likely include both a parking lot and an on-road portion to test a range of skills.

- An examiner will accompany you during testing without your adult driver present.

- The car you are testing in must have a current registration and proof of insurance in the car.

- The examiner will check your car for defects, like a cracked windshield or low tire pressure, before the road test.

- Before the test begins, you will be asked to activate controls such as headlights, taillights, turn signals, and windshield wipers, so be sure you know how to turn them on.

- Make sure your driver's education company gives you the certification of completion or uploads it to the Motor Vehicle Services website.

Road Test Skills

During the road test, the examiner will be looking to see if you can complete certain skills successfully. The good news is, these are all skills taught in driver's education and practiced during the required in-car instruction as well. There should be no surprises if you have studied your state manual and practiced. Here are some basic skills you should know.

Stopping

Examiners look for a full stop at stop signs. This includes stopping before the crosswalk, looking each way, gauging the position of other cars at the intersection, and then proceeding when safe. Stopping at a red light includes keeping a safe distance behind the car in front of you.

Standard Turns

The examiner will check that you use proper turn signals, stop before a right turn on red, yield to pedestrians or oncoming traffic, and obey signals with turn arrows or signage. You'll be graded on a variety of turns, including turns in the parking lot or on the way to the course.

Turn Signals

Using turn signals properly is often overlooked. You need to use a turn signal not only when executing turns, but also when entering parking spaces, changing lanes, or merging onto any road or highway. Also know whether your turn signal turns off automatically or needs manual deactivation. If you fail to deactivate the turn signal after your turn, you might lose points on the test.

Speed

Examiners will check your speed as you move through the test. It is important to maintain a steady speed without sudden accelerations or stops. Look for speed limit signs in case an examiner asks you for the current speed limit during the test and to ensure you are driving lawfully.

Following Distance

Maintaining a safe distance between cars is important whether you are driving in the suburbs, commercial areas, rural roads, or on the highway. Examiners will monitor your spacing and stopping distance. See chapter 1 for guidelines and tips on this topic to ensure you are not following cars too closely or unsafely.

Safety Measures

The examiner will check that your seat belt is buckled, you do not use the horn inappropriately, and you are focused on the road ahead. They may also check whether your windshield wipers or headlights are on, if necessary. If you need to, take a moment to stop, settle yourself, and mentally complete a safety checklist before you begin.

Lane Change

Changing lanes can be stressful under normal circumstances, and even more so on the test course. Practicing the steps involved can help. A successful lane change will include these steps: Turn on the appropriate turn signal, check your side mirror, turn your head to check your blind spot, move into the lane when safe, and finally turn off the turn signal.

Three-Point Turns

A three-point turn is used in narrow spaces where a U-turn is not possible. The examiner will look to see if you check the rearview mirror before reversing, if you turn the steering wheel properly, whether you make a full stop before changing gears, and that you do not bump into the curb or any obstacles when turning.

Optional Skills

The skills tested during a road test vary from state to state. For example, only some states test parallel parking, pulling straight into a parking space, backing out of a parking space, backing up on a straightaway, and backing up on a curve. It is your responsibility to know what is required on your state's road test.

Tips for Acing Your Road Test

I took the driving test more than forty years ago and still remember feeling nervous beforehand. I also recall being grateful I was prepared, because all that practice overtook my nerves at test time. There is no such thing as being "overprepared" for the road test. Not only will it take looking at your state's manual for the skills involved, but then you must put in the work in the real world. Drive every chance you get in all conditions and varying circumstances. Your goal is to make these skills automatic, which will help tremendously on test day and beyond.

BEFORE THE TEST

- Read the manual ahead of time and check off the skills required with practice notes.

- If you can't use the car you have been using for practice, allow extra time to get a feel for the car you will be driving on the road test.

- Ask questions of your in-car driver's education instructor. Oftentimes, they are familiar with the road test parameters.

- Wait to do the road test until you have mastered the skills. Attempting to test before you are prepared may damage your confidence in the long run.

- Many test courses are on YouTube, so check to see if yours is one of them.

- If possible, drive to the course and watch the test being administered on-site.

- If possible, determine the road portion of the test and drive the route to familiarize yourself.

- Notify your school or work in advance to get time off. Dashing around to get time off at the last minute will add unnecessary stress.

DAY OF THE TEST

- Get to your appointment fifteen minutes early.

- Make sure all your paperwork is in order so that you are not turned away.

- Turn off the radio once you arrive.

- Remember that the examiner wants you to pass. Disregard urban myths about examiners who "try to fail kids."

- Remember that you don't need a perfect score to pass. If you make a mistake, just refocus and move on.

- Make sure to be courteous and polite to everyone you encounter at the testing facility.

Part 2

SAFE, SMART, AND SKILLED DRIVING

CHAPTER 4

Cars 101

You are probably tired of me saying that driving is a big responsibility. So, I will switch it up. Cars are a responsibility, too! This is your go-to chapter for all things "car," from maintenance to alerts to features—I've got you covered.

Getting to Know a Car

A car is made up of complicated mechanical and computerized functions that are mostly under the hood and invisible to you. Everything works together to keep cars operating. Since no two cars are the same, it is important that you take time to get to know any car you will be driving. We will cover the areas you need to spend time investigating, like the dashboard, emergency brake, gas gauge, and speedometer. The owner's manual is your best resource for identifying warning lights, safety features, and recommended settings. Here are some things you can see, touch, and get to know:

GAS GAUGE: The gas gauge in your dashboard tells you how much gas is left in your tank. The gauge is typically marked with an "E" for empty, an "F" for full, and an arrow indicating the amount of fuel left. Get to know the markings, what kind of gas your car takes, and how many miles you have remaining if your gas light comes on. An electric car will have a battery icon that shows available miles instead of a gas gauge.

SPEEDOMETER: Also in the dashboard, the speedometer tells you how fast you are going. It is your job to know the speed limit and to slow down under certain weather conditions.

TURN SIGNALS: Turn on your signal lights to let other drivers know you are turning. Levers to turn them on and off are usually located on the side of the steering wheel.

HAZARD LIGHTS: The hazard lights are used when your car is not working properly. For instance, you should turn on the hazard lights if you have a flat tire and need to pull over to the side of the road to wait for assistance. The lights blink in both the front and back of the car in the same spot your turn signals light up. To activate them, there is usually a button to push or a tab to pull. Most are marked with a red or orange triangle.

EMERGENCY BRAKE: The emergency brake is an extra safeguard that stops the car when necessary. You use it in two general situations. The first is to keep a car from rolling on a hill when parked. The second is to stop the car in the rare case that the main braking system stops working. The emergency brake is different in all cars but can be a pedal on the floor near the regular brake pedal, or a handle that you pull. Never drive a car with the emergency brake activated. You should see a light on the dashboard that tells you the brake is on (see What Does That Light Mean? on page 71 for more information).

REARVIEW MIRROR: The rearview mirror is located at the center top of the windshield and should give you a clear view through the back window. It is important to check this mirror and adjust it, if necessary, every time you get in the car.

SIDEVIEW MIRRORS: These are two mirrors, one each located on the doors of the driver and the passenger and visible through the side window. If adjusted correctly, these mirrors give you a view of the road to each side of your car and should be checked before merging and changing lanes. When using sideview mirrors, always check your blind spot (see chapter 6, page 88) for cars not easily visible. Each car has a different mechanism for adjusting the mirrors, usually located on the door or near the mirrors. Both mirrors can be adjusted from the driver's side and all adjustments should be made before you start moving.

HEADLIGHTS: These are used to light your path and let other cars know where you are on the road. Some cars have automatic headlights that turn on if it is dark once the ignition is on. Other cars have a manual switch to turn on headlights. Check your owner's manual to see what type your car has. Cars also have a high beam setting for use in particular situations (see Headlights on page 59 for more information on high beams). The high beam switch is always manual, and can usually be turned on using a separate lever from the main headlight switch.

HEAT AND AIR-CONDITIONING SETTINGS: All cars have settings to regulate the temperature inside the car. This is usually a dial with red (heat) and blue (cold) markings to adjust the temperature. If your car has air-conditioning, a button, usually near the temperature dial, will turn it on. It is important to note that the air-conditioning is a separate system and can decrease your miles per gallon of gas, but the heat is generated through the warmth of the engine so you might not feel it immediately. The air-conditioning also works together with the defrost function.

DEFROST: The defrost system is used to clear the windows that fog up on the inside, or to defrost any ice covering the outside. A large volume of air blows through vents below your windshield to dry up condensation that forms when it's warmer in the car than it is outside. To clear ice or frost from the outside, the defroster blows warmer air from the engine to help melt it. Never wipe away condensation inside because it leaves smudges that make it hard to see through.

WINDSHIELD WIPERS: These sweep your windshield and keep it clear from rain, snow, and frost. Switches to turn on wipers are generally near the steering wheel, but each car is different. Some cars have both front and rear wipers with separate switches for each. Blades need to be replaced periodically, so you must pay attention to how effectively they are clearing the glass. Read more about windshield wipers and fluid later in Taking Care of Your Car (page 64).

DOOR LOCKS: Every car has a way of locking the car doors from the inside. Make note of whether your doors have a timing mechanism that locks doors automatically after a certain amount of time driving or if you need to lock them manually. Some cars have child safety locks that ensure the back doors can't be opened unless the driver unlocks them. Read the owner's manual to learn the different locking systems in your car.

WINDOW OPEN/CLOSE: Every car has a way of opening and closing the windows. Whether it is a manual cranking handle or automatic switches that toggle back and forth, get to know how the windows in your car operate. All windows should be closed every time you exit your car.

GAS AND HOOD RELEASE: Each car has a door on the gas tank keeping gas from getting contaminated. Some cars just have a door and others have a door with a fuel cap that needs to be unscrewed to access the tank. Learn where this door is located and how to open it. A hood release is also important to understand, especially if you experience car trouble and need to access the engine or battery. The hood release is on the driver's side, so check your owner's manual to see where it is exactly in your car.

DASHBOARD DETAILS

The dashboard is a communication center, like the home screen on your phone, with each part showing you something important. Gauges and lights can be confusing at first, but here are some must-know functions. Can you find them on your dashboard?

HEADLIGHT ILLUMINATION: Illuminates dashboard when headlights are on

TEMPERATURE GAUGES: Tracks the temperature of the coolant and engine and will alert you if the engine is too hot

BATTERY GAUGE: Tracks the car's battery charge

ODOMETER: Tracks your mileage for maintenance purposes

TACHOMETER: Measures the engine's rotation, mostly used with manual transmissions

TURN SIGNALS: Blink to show which way you are turning

CLOCK: Shows the current time and may need to be adjusted manually

VENTS: Adjust interior air flow

OUTDOOR TEMPERATURE: Displays outdoor temperature in some cars

NAVIGATION: Built-in screen in the dashboard for cars with navigation

Manual or Automatic?

The transmission of a car controls how engine power gets applied to the wheels. This involves shifting gears. All cars require drivers to use a gearshift to move into drive, reverse, neutral, or park. But cars also need different gears when moving. In general, first gear is used for big hills or towing. The second, third, and fourth gears are used for various kinds of suburban driving, whereas the fifth gear is used for driving fast, like on the highway.

Most cars use an automatic transmission that automatically switches between these driving gears based on speed and driving conditions. In an automatic transmission, the gearshift is between the passenger and driver's seat or on the steering wheel, and it is used only when the car is stopped to change to drive, neutral, reverse, or park.

Cars with manual transmissions require the driver to use a gearshift to switch gears by hand when driving. A manual gearshift is always located in the middle of the two front seats and works with a small pedal called a clutch, located near the brake pedal. It takes hours of training and practice to learn a manual shift. Never drive a manual transmission car without learning and practicing first because you can not only harm the transmission, but also cause a serious accident.

Electric Vehicles

Electric vehicles look like regular cars but have one very important difference: They do not use gas. Instead, electric cars need charging—like your phone or computer—to drive. Driving an electric car can be more complicated, but many choose to because it is more environmentally friendly. Without gasoline, electric cars do not put exhaust and fumes into the air we breathe. Additionally, electricity to power the cars can come from wind and solar power to preserve natural resources like oil. Maintenance costs of an electric car tend to be lower in the absence of oil changes or other engine tune-ups. However, electric cars can be more expensive to buy than gasoline vehicles and commercial chargers at gas stations and store parking lots charge a fee (see Charging Stations on page 90). Make sure to research these costs when deciding what type of car to buy. Always know what kind of car you are driving and whether it needs a charge or gas, and what type of gas it requires. Telltale signs of an electric car include the lack of an outer front grille, more legroom because of the battery placement, and lack of noise. Without the engine revving, electric cars are very quiet.

Hybrid Vehicles

A hybrid vehicle has a gasoline engine and at least one electric motor. These two systems work together to recapture energy and burn less gas. Burning less gas means you can go more miles per gallon and send less exhaust and pollution into the air. A separate battery pack gets charged through the braking system, as well as through the rotation of the engine, in the same way conventional gas engines charge the battery (see Taking Care of Your Car on page 64 for more on charging batteries). People choose hybrids if they want to help the environment but are not sure that charging the vehicle all the time is an option. The term "hybrid" covers a lot of different engine and battery combinations to power a car. Do your research with an adult if you want to buy a hybrid car. They also can be more expensive than a gas engine car, so if price is a factor, make sure you compare the cost savings over time.

Taking Care of Your Car

Car maintenance may be less fun than driving, but it's necessary to make your car last longer. Cars have recommended maintenance schedules usually based on mileage. For instance, your car's manual may say to change the oil every 5,000 miles you drive. Although some cars have lights and indicators to notify you if routine service is due, it is up to you to pay attention to mileage as well as sights and sounds of your car when you're driving. Keep music at a level where you can still hear your car switch gears, brake, and turn, and listen for maintenance and safety issues. Some common maintenance items include:

Oil Changes

In gas-powered cars, oil lubricates the engine and keeps the parts from grinding together and wearing down. So, changing your oil is an important part of car maintenance unless you have an electric car. Your manual will tell you how often to change the oil and oil filter to keep the engine in tip-top shape. After an oil change, the mechanic or garage usually puts a sticker on the upper left windshield that tells you when your next oil change is due. Although this is a huge help, it only works if you look at it every now and then and compare it to your mileage to see when it's time.

Tire Maintenance

Your tires balance your car and keep you driving safely on the road. A bad tire can affect turning and stopping and reduce your miles per gallon of gas. The car manual will tell you how much air should be in each tire and how often they should be rotated or switched from front to back and vice versa. Rotation is recommended because each tire wears differently, so switching them makes the tread wear out more evenly and last longer. Oftentimes, a mechanic will look at the tires when you go in for other routine maintenance and make a recommendation for rotation or replacement.

Battery

No matter what kind of vehicle you have, the battery is the heart of the car. When a new battery is installed, it comes with a warranty stating how long it should last with normal driving (see Car Terms on page 68 for more on warranties). So, if you leave the car idle for months when you are at college, the warranty won't cover a dead battery when you get home. If you are driving the car regularly, there are warning signs that the battery is losing charge. If you notice problems starting the car, dim lights, and your electric key fob not working, that might mean the battery needs to be checked. When in doubt, check the battery gauge on your dashboard and take it to a mechanic or dealership for testing.

Transmission Fluid

Transmission fluid coats the gears in your car so they don't grind and wear down over time. Cars are heavy, and changing gears to make all that weight speed up or slow down is tough work. Having the parts lubricated makes the process just a little easier. There are separate fluids for automatic transmissions and manual transmissions. As it works, the transmission fluid breaks down and gets contaminated with particles, so check the manual for recommended change intervals.

Brakes

Nothing is scarier than the thought of your brakes failing when driving. It happened to me as an adult, and I will share what I learned. I discovered that the signs of brake failure had been there, but I just didn't recognize them. If you have to push down hard on the brake pedal to stop, or notice a squeaking or grinding sound, it means that the brakes need to be looked at by a professional. Make a plan to test the brakes every six months when having the tires checked and rotated. Keep maintenance on a schedule for things like brakes and brake fluid to prevent an emergency.

Front-End Alignment

Ideally, your tires and front end will both travel in a straight line if the wheel is not turned. But everyday occurrences—like encountering potholes or bumping into the curb on a turn or when parking—can affect your car's alignment. One of the first signs a car is not aligned is if the car "pulls" to the right or left. This means the suspension that supports the wheels and steering column are not in sync. Have a professional check your alignment at least once a year to help your tires last longer and keep you safer.

Filters

Most cars have four filters that work to keep it running smoothly. An oil filter keeps the car's oil free of dirt and contaminants, which keeps the engine efficient. The air filter is a workhorse! It is responsible for keeping bugs, dirt, rocks, and any debris from entering the engine through the car's front grille. Fuel filters protect the gasoline in your car from contaminants that could harm the engine. Lastly, the cabin filter works inside the car to rid the air of dust and dirt. All these filters need to be checked regularly. Your manual will make recommendations for changing them.

Car Wash

This may sound silly, but washing your car really is part of maintenance, especially in the winter when salt and snow coat cars. Exterior care is just as important as maintenance under the hood. Regular car washes preserve the paint on the car, can make light scratches less noticeable, makes the filters' jobs easier, and keeps the car looking fresh, which is important when you want to sell your car. And a hand wash is just as beneficial as paying for a professional car wash, so this does not have to be expensive.

Choosing a Mechanic

Finding a mechanic you trust is sometimes difficult. Work with trusted adults to identify a mechanic who is familiar with your type of vehicle and has a good reputation with good customer reviews. Although price should be a consideration, sometimes you get what you pay for. So, if a mechanic is much cheaper than others, it could be a red flag that they are not competent. Recommendations and referrals are more important here. Also, mechanics can be independent, part of a dealership, have a shop in a gas station, or be a part of a national chain like Jiffy Lube that provides car service. It may take some trial and error to find the right person, but as long as they provide quality work at a price you can afford, it doesn't matter where they are located.

Car Terms

Talking shop with a mechanic can seem intimidating, but only if you don't know the lingo. To ensure you are explaining what your car needs, learn the terms below:

RPM: Short for revolutions per minute, this indicates how many times your engine turns per minute. RPM is primarily used in manual transmission cars.

JUMP START: Refers to the battery of one car giving a "jump" to the dead battery in another car. Hooking cables to the batteries in each car is dangerous and requires training. Never attempt this alone.

ABS: Short for anti-lock brake system, which helps stop skidding when stopping suddenly.

PSI: Short for pounds per square inch, this refers to how much air should always be in your tires. The PSI level is listed in your manual.

CLUTCH: A pedal that connects the engine with the transmission in manual transmission cars.

GEARSHIFT: The lever or handle that is adjusted to move the car between gears in both automatic and manual transmission.

MPG: Short for miles per gallon, it represents how many miles you can drive on one gallon of gasoline.

AWD: Short for all-wheel drive, this refers to cars that have balanced power in all four wheels to help with traction.

WARRANTY: The car and its parts have warranties stating how long they should last under normal circumstances. If a part is under warranty and breaks, you do not have to pay for it, so check for warranties before repair.

JACK AND LUG NUTS: These are two basic tools for changing a tire. A jack is a device with a foot pump and platform to raise the car for easier access to the tire. Lug nuts attach wheels to the axle and must come off before a tire can be changed. If you have never changed tires before, get help from an adult.

Troubleshooting

There are some issues you'll come across no matter what kind of car you drive. Though these issues are common, they still need the expertise of a professional mechanic who can diagnose the issue and has access to the right parts to correct it. It is not safe to try to make these repairs yourself! Always speak with an adult or mechanic about what the car is doing or which warning lights you see. Here are some issues you might run into:

SQUEAKING OR GRINDING BRAKES: If you hear squeaking or grinding when you brake, that is a sign your brakes are wearing out and may need replacing. Once you hear this noise, do not wait to have this looked at—take it straight to a repair shop. Malfunctioning brakes are a danger to you and other drivers.

CAR PULLS TO ONE SIDE: Part of driving is "feeling" the car. On the highway, does the car drift slightly one way unless you firmly guide it to stay straight? This means the car is out of alignment and the tires need to be checked as soon as possible.

NOISE WHEN CHANGING GEARS: You should not hear anything when your car shifts from one gear to another. If there is a clunk or you feel a lurch, have your transmission checked.

WIPERS NOT CLEARING: If there are streaks on your windshield and water or snow is not clearing, you need new blades. Don't let this slide; a blurry windshield is dangerous.

STEERING WHEEL SHAKING: If you feel vibration or shaking in the steering wheel, it might be your wheels and the suspension that holds them that need to be checked.

HEADLIGHTS: Occasionally, you should check your headlights and taillights when not out driving. You can be stopped by the police for these malfunctions. If a headlight or taillight bulb is out, get it fixed as soon as possible.

OVERHEATING: If your temperature gauge moves to the hot side, or you notice steam coming from under the hood, your car is overheating. Turn off the engine and let the car cool down. Do not drive an overheated car, and discuss what's happening with an adult.

ENGINE WON'T START: If your engine sounds like it wants to start but won't, it can be either a dead battery or a bad alternator, which gives power to the battery. Charge or jump-start the battery. If the car starts, problem solved. If not, it is likely the alternator and a mechanic needs to repair it.

GRINDING OR WHINING WHEN TURNING: If you hear a grinding noise when turning, you are low on power steering fluid or have a power steering problem. Both conditions affect your ability to turn safely and need immediate attention.

LOOSE FUEL CAP: This seems like no big deal, but if the fuel cap won't seal it can affect an emissions test result, contaminate the gas in the car, and lead to poor gas mileage. A mechanic can fix or replace a fuel cap.

WHAT DOES THAT LIGHT MEAN?

The dashboard has tools to alert you to a malfunction or problem. Here are some common icons you may see:

 SEAT BELT: Buckle the driver's or passengers' seat belts immediately.

 LOW TIRE PRESSURE: Have an adult or mechanic check immediately for a flat tire or one that needs air.

 FUEL: Fuel is low, so stop and get gas. Do not attempt to drive with the fuel light on.

 HIGH BEAMS: Indicates high beams are on. See Headlights on page 15 for more info.

 BRAKE WARNING: Emergency brake is on or the braking system needs immediate attention.

 ENGINE CHECK: The engine needs to be checked by a mechanic immediately.

 OIL: Low oil pressure needs immediate attention.

 BATTERY: Battery charge is low and needs immediate attention.

 AIRBAG: Only shows when airbag systems are not working. Check immediately.

 TEMPERATURE: Risk of overheating and needs immediate attention.

CARS 101

That was a lot of information to take in! Feel free to come back to this chapter anytime you need a quick reference or reminder. Here are our main takeaways:

→ Learn common car terms and which of them applies to your car.

→ Know the difference between electric, hybrid, and gas engine cars.

→ Learn your dashboard by reading your manual.

→ Follow the maintenance schedule for your car.

→ Pay attention to your car's sights and sounds.

→ Always let a professional repair your car.

→ Warning lights should never be ignored.

→ When in doubt, ask an adult to determine if there is an issue with your car.

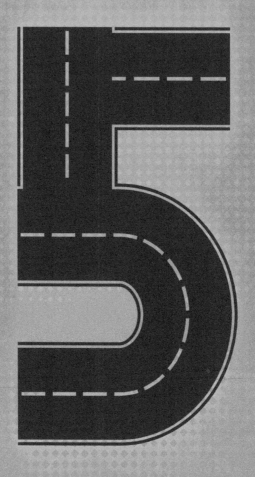

CHAPTER 5

Before You Get on the Road

You've probably been a passenger in a car and thought driving looked easy, and almost effortless. It's easy to overlook how much time, practice, and studying went into making it look that way. Being road ready takes work and preparation. In this chapter, you will learn the most important things to know before you drive, including challenges you may face and documents you need. Trust me, one day you will make driving look effortless, too!

Know Your GDL Rules

The Graduated Driver Licensing (GDL) rules are the first step in becoming a driver. Although the details vary from state to state, every state has a GDL system in place. What is it exactly?

The GDL lays out the milestones necessary to qualify for licensure in your state. It includes rules about driver's education classes, skills you will be required to know on the road test, and how many in-car practice hours you need.

A big part of the GDL process is the adult driver who will oversee your driving process, in addition to the required driving instruction from a certified course and instructor. In almost every state, an adult driver will coach you as a new driver and reinforce the rules of the road. In some states, these coaches are required to sign a practice log with a minimum number of hours driving on all kinds of roadways and in all weather conditions. Never shortcut these regulations because they are in place for your safety and the safety of other drivers on the road.

Never Drive under the Influence

Almost every state has a zero-tolerance policy for driving under the influence of alcohol or drugs. Let's review how to navigate situations where drugs and alcohol might be present.

Alcohol

According to the National Highway Traffic Safety Administration (NHTSA), "alcohol is a substance that reduces the function of the brain, impairing thinking, reasoning, and muscle coordination. All these abilities are essential to operating a vehicle safely."

Each state determines its own legal limits for alcohol, but this should not be interpreted as a green light to drink even a little bit. States use calculations called blood alcohol concentration (BAC) to test the amount of alcohol in your bloodstream. If the BAC is above a certain level, you are considered intoxicated. You have no way of knowing how your body responds to alcohol, processes it, or rids it from your system. The only way to avoid intoxication is to not drink. Two violations result from drinking and driving. Driving under the influence (DUI) is a lesser charge given if you have a smaller concentration of alcohol in your bloodstream. Driving when intoxicated (DWI) is a more serious infraction as the concentration of alcohol in your bloodstream is higher.

Drugs

Many drugs, legal and illegal, can impair your ability to drive. It is easy to assume that known drugs like marijuana and cocaine are the only ones to avoid. However, prescription drugs or over-the-counter drugs can also impair driving. Always read warning labels on prescription and over-the-counter drugs before taking them if you're planning to drive.

It is illegal to drive under the influence of marijuana even in states that have legalized marijuana use. Moreover, don't let the lack of a roadside test for marijuana (like there is for alcohol) fool you. Trained professionals know what to look for, and lying to the police to try and cover for marijuana use when driving is punishable by law.

Handling Tricky Situations

Sometimes you may encounter situations where substances that alter your system are available whether you are driving or a passenger. Plan for these circumstances by walking through options with a trusted adult. Is there a designated driver? Is there a rideshare app you can use to take you home? Can an adult come pick you up?

The most important thing to remember is that impaired people have trouble recognizing they are impaired. Do not let them sway you or negotiate with you. Never drive impaired or ride with an impaired driver, even if it means taking away someone's keys or reporting behavior to a trusted adult or authority. In many states, Good Samaritan laws allow a minor to involve the police or medical personnel if another minor needs assistance due to the effects of drugs or alcohol without fear of getting in trouble themselves.

Designated Drivers

A designated driver is an individual who agrees to abstain from alcohol or drugs for the evening to safely drive others who may be impaired. Having a designated driver in no way excuses underage drinking or drinking to excess for passengers. Designated drivers should be aware of the condition of everyone in their vehicle. They should also encourage their group to drink responsibly. It is important to know that most states do not allow teens with permits to act as designated drivers for adults over the age of twenty-one who have had any amount of alcohol or drugs.

Keep These in the Car

There are unpleasant realities to driving, such as emergencies, getting pulled over by the police, or experiencing an accident. None of these incidents automatically means that you've done anything wrong. But if it happens, being prepared will help you navigate the situation without making it more stressful. Here are some documents and tools you should have when driving. The first three documents are what a police officer will ask to see when you are pulled over for any reason, so you must always have them when driving:

DRIVER'S LICENSE: Your driver's license is your identification not only when driving but also whenever you need to prove who you are. Licenses have a unique assigned number used to check for your violations and driving record if pulled over. This sounds scarier than it is; usually it just proves that you have no outstanding tickets or anything that is a problem.

REGISTRATION: All cars must be registered as proof of ownership in the state where the legal owners live. The registration state must match the state of the license plates on the car, and both must be renewed on time. Registrations have staggered expirations and vary from state to state. You should know where the registration is kept in every car you drive, whether it is yours or borrowed. The registration is a way of verifying that the car is yours or that you have permission to drive it in the event of an accident or a traffic stop.

INSURANCE CARD: Cars must also be insured in almost every state. Generally, car insurance covers costs that might need to be paid to fix your car or other cars and/or to get medical attention for yourself or other drivers in case of an accident. Insurance is complicated; you are essentially paying money up front every year (called a premium) as a down payment on money the company would pay if you had an accident or claim. The two main types of insurance are "collision," which covers accidents, and "comprehensive," which covers other things like a tree falling on a car. Speak with a guardian about insurance and don't navigate it by yourself. Each state requirement is different, and having an insurance agent you trust is important.

OWNER'S MANUAL: We covered some basics of the car in chapter 4, but even after you familiarize yourself with it, the owner's manual that comes with the vehicle should be handy as a refresher.

TIRE CHANGE KIT: Knowing how to change a tire is an essential skill. Keep a spare tire, jack, and any lug nut tools in the car in the event of a flat tire. Practice changing your tire in a safe place a few times so when it happens in an emergency, you are prepared.

FLASHLIGHT AND FLARES: The flashlight is invaluable for car trouble after dark. Flares for warning other drivers are a good idea, too. Also, don't forget to check the batteries occasionally and switch them out if they lose their charge.

JUMPER CABLES: You can recharge a dead battery with jumper cables or a portable charging station you can buy.

Charging can be dangerous as it involves live voltage from another car used to "jump" your battery. Do not attempt to charge a car without supervision. Once a battery needs to be jumped, it should be tested by a professional in case the battery needs to be replaced.

AUTO CLUB CARD: If you, your family, or guardian has an auto club card that assists in roadside emergencies, keep this card available in your wallet, the glove compartment, or the center console in case of an emergency. Auto clubs are good for towing, fixing flat tires, and charging or changing batteries.

WINTER WEATHER KIT: If driving in the winter, it is a good idea to keep blankets, water, a few nonperishable snacks, and a phone charging block in the trunk. Slick roads cause pileups and accidents. If you are stuck in a backup or stranded, these will sustain you until help arrives or you get moving.

Buckle Up

When I was a kid, there were no seat belt laws. I can remember bouncing around the car every time we hit a bump or sharp turn. Fortunately, we never had an accident, but it felt unsafe even then. Thank goodness seat belt use today is regulated in nearly every state, and we have the data to prove it saves lives.

You as a driver are responsible for making sure everyone in the car is buckled up. I have refused to drive a carpool if even one passenger won't use a seat belt. It is your duty to refuse to drive if passengers will not wear their seat belts, too. A good rule to follow is that any time a seat belt is provided, it needs to be used. That includes rideshares, taxis, multi-passenger vans, or buses.

Just as important as remembering to buckle up is to properly position the seat belt so it can protect you if you need it. The lap belt should be tight across your hips, and the shoulder strap should start on your outside shoulder and cross your chest diagonally.

Make sure to research the seat belt laws in your state and then enforce them every time you are in the car.

HOW TO HOLD A STEERING WHEEL

It is easy to think of the steering wheel like a clock. When facing the steering wheel, your right hand should be on the "3" of the clock and your left hand on the "9." This position keeps you balanced and in full control of the wheel. It is never okay to "palm" the steering wheel, which is putting your palm in the center and turning the wheel. Driving with only one hand is also not safe. Many examiners take note of these hand positions as part of the road test.

Phone Use

One of the biggest challenges of becoming a safe driver is managing phone use. According to CarInsurance.com, about 39.2 percent of teens nationwide text when driving. The CDC further explains that texting takes your eyes off the road for about five seconds. If you're driving at 55 mph, your car can travel the equivalent of an entire football field in those five seconds.

Imagine driving the car down a block in your neighborhood with your eyes closed. That sounds crazy and dangerous, right? Yet, that is essentially what happens when you send a text when driving. Texting uses your brain, eyes, and hands simultaneously, so that major shift in focus can be deadly. Is any text worth suffering lifelong consequences like serious injury or even death?

Texting when driving is illegal in almost every state, including texting at a stoplight, in traffic, or using a smart watch. The tough part is balancing the value of a phone with safety. Using a hands-free phone to make a call and a voice-to-text message could be technically allowed in your state, but it's still a form of distracted driving that comes with serious risk. Just like buckling your seat belt, managing cell phone use must be automatic for drivers. Much of driving is planning, and a phone can help this process. The trick is not compromising focus while utilizing those apps that can help you when driving. Here are tips for finding that balance:

NAVIGATION: Set the destination before leaving and choose voice prompts or a phone mount to use navigation without looking at the phone. If you get lost or confused, do not attempt to adjust on the fly; pull off the road and reset.

PLAYLIST: Select music before leaving and resist the urge to skip songs and manage the selections.

HANDS-FREE CALLING: Many cars are equipped with hands-free calling. However, all calls should wait until you arrive at your destination.

SILENCE NOTIFICATIONS: Turn on "do not disturb" mode before driving or make sure to silence all notifications when you drive.

AUTOMATIC MESSAGING APP: Download an app that automatically responds to texts and calls with a message that says you are driving and will answer when you can. This avoids repeat calls and texts.

MAKE SURE ADULTS KNOW WHEN YOU'RE DRIVING: Studies show that worried adults often call kids when they are driving, which can be a distraction. Talk about this with the adults in your life and form a communication plan.

Finally, be the example even if no one else around you follows safe phone use during driving.

Other Distractions

One of my sons crashed into a neighbor's parked car because a spider dropped in front of him. It never occurred to me to add bugs to the list of driving distractions, but unexpected things can happen on the road.

A distraction is anything that takes your focus away from driving and increases risk. Distractions come from issues inside the car or out on the road. It is your job to expect distractions and prepare for them. Distractions that are out of your control, like weather and accidents, can happen any time.

FRIENDS: Many GDL systems limit passengers for beginner drivers. They also have rules about who the passengers can be (for example, only family members). When driving others, it is your responsibility to set the tone for safe behavior before passengers get in the car with you. Passengers should not distract you by making loud noises, moving around the car, or anything else that takes your eyes off the road.

PETS: Pets should be in the car only if they are restrained. They are unpredictable, distracting, and can easily cause an accident. If you can, have a passenger in the car with you to help in case the pet needs assistance or is in distress.

FOOD: It is impossible to practice safe driving and eat at the same time because both hands cannot be on the wheel when eating. It is much safer to pull over to eat, eat before leaving, or eat after you arrive at your destination.

MUSIC: Driving may be more enjoyable with music, but it cannot be at the cost of safe driving. If using a playlist on a device, set it before you hit the road. If you are relying on the radio, change the channel only if you can do so without taking your eyes off the road. Is good music worth an accident? Never! It is always better to plan entertainment ahead of time.

ACCIDENTS: It sounds backward to say accidents are distracting but hear me out. It can be very jarring to see an accident when driving. Resist the urge to turn and look—called rubbernecking—because it takes your eyes off the road in front of you and could cause you to slow down. Accidents that happen because of existing accidents are more common than you would think.

AIR AND HEAT SETTINGS: Get familiar with how to change the dials to adjust temperature or turn on the defrost. You should be able to do this without taking your eyes off the road. See chapter 4 (page 58) for more about getting to know your car and its settings.

VIDEO OR MOVIES: Many vehicles are equipped with passenger screens for movies. Screens should never be adjusted so the driver can see it when driving. Also, never try to start a video or movie for passengers when driving. Do this when parked or before leaving.

LAST STEPS: A CHECKLIST

Before hitting the road, here are some last steps to check:

- ☐ Your wallet, with your license in it, needs to be with you any time you drive.

- ☐ Adjust car settings, including checking mirrors, seat, seat belt, and steering wheel position.

- ☐ Lock doors if they don't lock automatically before pulling out.

- ☐ Make sure you have enough gas or electric battery charge to get you where you are going, or plan to stop on the way.

- ☐ Check your route for tolls and have a plan to pay if there are any.

- ☐ Set your destination on the navigation app before you leave (see Phone Use on page 82) and check for traffic delays.

- ☐ Make sure to have a communication plan so someone knows where you are going and when you are expected to arrive.

- ☐ Set up any music devices so no adjustments will be necessary when driving (see Other Distractions on page 83).

CHAPTER 6

On the Road

Because you are not always in control of what's on the road, driving can be unpredictable. Other drivers, bad road conditions, weather events, and mechanical problems—any of these could change your driving experience at any moment. Knowing some of the obstacles and how to navigate them if they arise will take the stress out of being on the road. In this chapter, you'll get an overview of situations you might encounter when driving and how to handle them.

Things to Watch Out For

You learned in chapter 5 (page 75) about the importance of staying focused when driving. Although you should *always* be alert behind the wheel, here are some situations when you need to pay extra attention:

TRAFFIC JAMS: When traffic is slow, it might seem okay to play with the radio or lose focus, but the opposite is true. You need to remain focused and ready to react. Slow traffic can frustrate drivers, causing them to change lanes quickly. If traffic happens due to an accident, emergency vehicles may approach on the shoulder.

DRIVING ON UNFAMILIAR ROADS: Most of your driving will be back and forth to school, work, extracurricular activities, and to see friends—in other words, on familiar roads. If you find yourself on a new road, read signs for the speed limit and adjust your speed to the flow of traffic. If you feel uncomfortable, you can drive slightly slower than the speed limit.

RUNNING LATE: When you are running late, it is tempting to drive too fast and take shortcuts to save time. You won't save any time if you have an accident or get stopped by police. Either allow enough time to get to your destination or let someone know you are running late before you leave.

BLIND SPOTS: Blind spots are the areas around your car that aren't visible through the mirrors or windows. You must turn your head and look over your shoulder to check for cars in that blind spot before switching lanes or merging into traffic. Be mindful of when you might be in another driver's blind spot and move up or back a little to become more visible.

GETTING LOST: Sometimes the navigation takes you the wrong way or you might miss a turn, but do not let emotion take over. Stay focused and look at your surroundings for familiar things or wait for navigation to autocorrect. If the navigation can't redirect you immediately, find a parking lot or side street to pull over and find directions.

DRIVING A NEW CAR: If you're driving an unfamiliar car, take extra care until you see how the car handles. Are the brakes touchy? Does the gas pedal stick? Is it bigger and needs more room for steering? Where are the wipers and the horn?

DIGITAL MESSAGE BOARDS: Permanent digital signs can be hanging above highways. You might also see portable speed and closure warnings in suburban areas. These messages can be important, but it can be difficult to read when driving. It is okay to slow down a little to scan the sign as soon as you can see it and look for key words like "alert" or "warning." If there is a warning, read as much as you can and follow directions. If it is a reminder to slow down or buckle up, these are useful, too.

Getting Gas

There are two kinds of gas stations: full service, where an attendant pumps the gas, and self-service, where you pump it yourself. In some states, there is no self-service, so make sure you read all signs when you stop for gas in a new area. Most cars take unleaded gas (not diesel), but check your manual to confirm. You are likely to see three different types of gas: regular (least expensive), super (more expensive), and premium (most expensive). Talk to your mechanic or an adult who knows your car about the best gas to use.

- Walk around the outside of the car to identify the door to the gas tank. Then once at the station, pull your car up to a pump on the same side as the door to your gas tank. If you are paying cash, go inside the station and the clerk will help you.

- If paying by credit card, you can usually do that at the pump, but if it is too confusing, you can go inside.

- Make sure the fuel door is open and the gas cap is off so you can insert the hose.

- The pump screen will clear the number of gallons and dollars to zero. You should see a message that says something like "lift handle and select fuel." This means the pump is ready. When the pump is ready, lift the handle of the fuel hose, push the button for the grade of fuel you want to buy, and insert the hose into the fuel tank.

- Once the hose is in, push the lever inside the handle of the hose to release the gas. You should hear the pump activate and feel the gas in the hose. The pump will automatically stop pumping when your tank is full. Do not push the lever after the pump indicates a full tank; overfilling is not good for the car. If you have prepaid, the pump will shut off when the allotted dollar amount has been reached, regardless of whether the tank is full or not.

SAFETY

- If you need to go into the gas station minimart for snacks or the bathroom, move your car to a parking space first.

- Never leave the pump running and go inside. Always stay with your car until you have finished your transaction.

- Lastly, make sure to keep your keys with you as you pay and pump, and lock the doors if you leave the car at the pump to pay inside.

Charging Stations

If you're driving an electric vehicle (EV), you will need to find a charging station instead of a gas station. You can use apps to find local charging stations and to see how much they cost.

There are different charging levels for EVs. Level 1 is the most common, which you can often do through a converter kit for regular household outlets. There is no additional charge outside of your electric bill, but this method takes the longest to charge. On average, one hour of Level 1 charging equals three to seven miles of driving. If you are not going far, this type of charging is ideal.

Level 2 charging is faster, averaging twenty to thirty miles for every hour of charging. Level 2 chargers are for home use, but you must buy them and have them installed by an electrician, which can be expensive.

Lastly, Level 3 charging is found in most public charging stations. It is the fastest, taking a battery from 0 to 80 percent in roughly thirty minutes. You pay fees for using a public charger.

Driving in Different Settings

It is always important to follow the basic rules of the road no matter where you are, but some driving situations have unwritten rules. Here are some lesser-known rules you should know:

Driving in Traffic

Driving in traffic can be stressful. More cars on the road requires more focus. The most important thing is to pay attention to speed. Encountering traffic often means you will be traveling below the speed limit. This is a good thing! It gives you extra time to stop if needed and makes it easier for other cars to merge. Pick a lane and stay in it. Switching lanes frequently in heavy traffic ups the chances of an accident. Be aware of not only your blind spot but the blind spots of other drivers. Do not sit in the blind spot of another vehicle; reposition your vehicle to make your car more visible. Give yourself plenty of time to get to your turn or exit. Waiting until the last minute to move over can be dangerous. Lastly, use signals to announce your intentions to other drivers. Other drivers are focused on their own merges, exits, and lane changes, so warning them of your intention helps everyone. Driving in traffic means you need to be more cautious and practice defensive driving.

Driving in Rural Areas

The country can be beautiful, but it has unique driving challenges. Rural roads can be winding with no real shoulder. There is very little margin for error before you either cross the center line or land in a ditch or field. That means slow and steady is the way to go. Maintain a speed that fits your comfort level, at or just below the speed limit. If a car wants to pass you, simply slow down and let them pass in front of you.

Remote roads also have fewer streetlights. If driving at night, slow your speed and use high beam headlights if no cars are approaching. Signage can be less obvious on rural roads, so you may need extra work on navigation. For instance, if you see a sign saying your turn is in five miles, look at the clock and note that in about five minutes you need to start anticipating that turn. Wildlife is also an added risk in rural areas as we are driving through their natural habitat. Scan the horizon for movement to identify animals. Stay alert because where there is one animal, there are often more.

Driving in Cities

The biggest challenge to driving in a city is all the activity! Pedestrians, buses, and rideshares all compete for space and your attention. The good news is speed limits are lower in cities, giving you more reaction time. Before driving in the city, look at your route on a navigation system if you can. Find out ahead of time if there are any one-way streets, turn-only lanes, and no-turn-on-red lights in your route. Knowing what to expect will make it easier to handle any tricky obstacles.

Although pedestrians should stay in crosswalks, they often do not (see more on pedestrians in chapter 1, page 8). It is your responsibility to watch for people stepping off the curb. Intersections (also covered in depth in chapter 1, page 11) require focus and defensive driving, or watching for others making driving errors. One of the most common mistakes drivers make is speeding up to make it through a yellow light before it turns red. Watch for cars like this when making a left across oncoming traffic, before you proceed. As a side note, parking in the city can be confusing with multiple signs stacked near each other. So, when in doubt, move on and find a parking lot or a space with clear signage about restrictions.

Driving at Night

Your field of vision can be limited at night. Your low beam headlights light up the road about 200 feet ahead, which is approximately two-thirds the length of a football field. On a well-lit road, like on a highway or in the city, 200 feet is plenty. However, when driving through darker, more rural areas, your high beams will project another 100 feet or so. If no other driver is approaching from the opposite direction, the high beams are a huge help. Headlights can make it hard to judge how far a car is from you, so allow extra time for stops, turns, and merges at night. Nighttime driving means you are constantly adjusting to different types of light as you travel. Headlights, streetlights, taillights, and traffic signals all come and go. One minute you might be driving in relative darkness and the next an oncoming car's headlights are piercing the night ahead. This constant shift in vision can tire your eyes. One way to lessen this is to make sure your windshield is clear. Smears and streaks distort light and make it harder to see overall.

Driving in Different Weather Conditions

The safest plan is to avoid driving when the weather makes the roads dangerous. However, sometimes you are already on the road when bad weather arrives, and you can't avoid it. Here are some strategies for navigating bad weather safely.

Rain

Rain makes it hard to see and reduces traction of your tires on the road, especially when it first begins raining. Roads build up oil and dirt over time. When it first starts to rain, that oil and water mix to make the surface very slick, making cars more likely to skid. After it has rained for a while, the oil washes away and the road becomes less slippery. If you're on the road when it first starts raining, you need to slow down and leave more following distance. Driving in the rain will be easier if your windshield wipers and tires are working and in good shape. Traveling too fast in the rain can cause hydroplaning (see sidebar on page 95, How to Handle Hydroplaning), which can be especially dangerous for new drivers to handle. Braking in the rain should never be sudden, but rather gentle and steady.

Remember "turn around, don't drown," which means that you should not drive through large puddles or road flooding because it can be life-threatening. In heavy rains, bridges and roads that curve and dip are most likely to have standing water. If you can avoid these areas in heavy rain, you should. If not, look for signs warning of standing water and road closures and reverse course if you need to. Turn headlights on in the rain even if it is not required by your state laws.

HOW TO HANDLE
HYDROPLANING

Hydroplaning occurs when there is a layer of water between your tires and the road. It makes your tires lose contact with the road and makes you unable to steer effectively. It is the result of speed, weather, tire condition, water depth, and the road itself. Any combination of those things can cause hydroplaning. So, what do you do? When you feel you are losing control from hydroplaning, immediately shift the car into neutral ("N" on the gearshift). Then, put on your emergency flashers and keep the steering wheel straight so the wheels are pointed forward. When you regain traction, shift to drive, turn off your flashers, and slow your speed to prevent it from happening again.

Snow and Ice

Many of the same strategies for navigating rain—maintaining safe speeds and no quick braking—apply for snow and ice as well. Maintaining your tires, windshield wipers, and antifreeze helps keep you safe, just like stowing items in your car in case you get stranded due to a storm (see Keep These in the Car on page 78). If you get caught in sleet or snow, slow down, watch for cars stopped or stuck in bad conditions, and go straight to your destination. You should use headlights not only to help you see, but to let other cars see you. If you become stranded, do not walk for help or stand outside the car. Stay inside and call a trusted adult or roadside service if you have it. Don't forget to use the car's defrost feature to keep the inside windshield clear.

Remember that bridges and overpasses freeze first because the cold air under the structure freezes the precipitation on the road. The most important skill for snow and ice is handling a skid. A skid is a loss of tire traction causing the car to slide or move without steering. If your car starts skidding, remain calm and follow these steps:

1. Remove your foot from the gas.

2. Do not brake hard.

3. Gently turn the steering wheel in the direction the car is swerving.

4. Then tap the brakes lightly until you regain traction.

Fog

Fog severely limits your vision, so it is best to stay off the road until it clears, if possible. It is caused by an extreme difference in air and ground temperature, so the condensation settles at low altitudes. If you must be on the road in fog, slow down, increase following distance, use only your low beam headlights, and never stop on the road in the fog. Because of low visibility, other cars may not see you if stopped, which is very dangerous. Usually, fog burns off as temperatures rise, so if you can wait to head out, it will be safer.

Floods

Driving through standing water can be life-threatening, so it is better to turn around. Contrary to what you might think, flooding can happen very quickly if a lot of rain falls in a short period of time. Many areas prone to flooding will be marked with a yellow Flood Zone sign. Make note if you see this sign when driving in the rain. If a road is closed due to flooding, slowly follow the directive of officials or signs, and find a well-lit, public place to pull over if you need navigation.

How Heat and Cold Can Affect a Car

Most cars are designed to operate through changes in temperatures and varying climates. However, extreme weather conditions can affect your car. For instance, freezing temperatures can affect your tire pressure. This makes it difficult to decipher whether the tires are low or just reacting to the weather. Always monitor how they look and feel, and any warning lights, to see that they recalibrate as the temperature rises throughout the day.

Cold weather also affects car batteries by thickening all the fluids that keep a battery charged. Having jumper cables ready in cold weather is a good idea.

Freezing temperatures can cause car doors to freeze shut and all your windows to ice over. Never use anything but the heat of the engine and a scraper on the windows. For frozen doors, often just pushing on the door seam with your body is enough to break up ice.

Very hot weather can be hard on cars as well. The tires and batteries are susceptible to extreme heat when hot pavements and overheated engine fluids wreak havoc. Make regular visits to the mechanic if you often experience extreme temperatures.

PROTECT YOUR PETS!

Never leave an animal in your car unattended. According to the American Kennel Club (AKC), the inside of a car parked in 70 degree weather can reach 100 degrees in just twenty minutes. Cracking a window for air does little to change the temperature. The AKC also states that hundreds of dogs die from heatstroke every year. This led many states to enact laws restricting people from leaving pets unattended in cars. When driving, protect pets in a crate, harness, or carrier.

What to Do If . . .

When you leave the house, you never think you are going to have an emergency on the road (accident or mechanical problem), get stopped, or get a ticket. Rest assured, almost everyone experiences these things occasionally. Stay calm if you run into issues. The important thing in emergencies and unexpected situations is taking accountability. Did the car break down because of lack of maintenance? Did you get a ticket because you were speeding? Although these events are common, they will be much less frequent if you are acting as a responsible driver. Here are situations and tips to navigate them:

You Have Car Trouble

If you are lucky, a warning light or gauge will alert you to impending mechanical issues, allowing you time to pull over safely or avoid driving. But what happens if your issue is sudden and unavoidable?

First, stay calm and remember that most of your car is working even if one function is not. All those parts are pulling together to get you to safety.

Secondly, put on your hazard lights as soon as you can. This alerts drivers you are slowing down and may need to move over to the shoulder or exit the roadway. Once stopped safely, it is important to know what you don't know. This means do not attempt to fix the car yourself unless the problem is obvious and simple to repair, like a flat tire if you have been trained. If the problem is unclear or you can't fix it, call either a trusted adult or an auto club if you have one. Describe what you felt, saw, or smelled in the car as best you can.

Next, place any flares or warning devices you may have out on the road behind your car. If you are waiting for someone to meet you, exit the car and move a safe distance away along the tree line if there is one. This protects you in the unlikely event a moving car hits yours when it is stopped. Keep your phone and wallet/purse with you.

You Get Pulled Over

The sight of a police cruiser behind you with lights flashing is enough to make anyone's heart race, regardless of how experienced a driver you are. There is no way to tell whether you are the one being stopped unless you move over to make way for the police car to pass. If the police follow your lane changes, you are being stopped, and you must keep moving to the right until it is safe to come to a stop.

It is important to stay in the car and wait for the officer to approach you. Roll down the window to speak with the officer, but don't open the door, and keep your hands on the steering wheel. If the officer asks for your license and registration, you will have a moment to get them, but knowing where these items are ahead of time will lead to less fumbling in a nervous moment.

You can greet the officer respectfully, but do not ask any questions until you have been informed why you are being stopped. In these cases, the less you say the better. If you were speeding, do not try to explain that you are late. If you have a taillight that is not working (yes, you can be pulled over for that), don't say that you've been meaning to get that fixed. If you need clarification or more information, for instance, how far over the speed limit you were going, you may ask after the officer has finished speaking or if prompted. The more polite and respectful you are, the better the experience will be.

You Get a Ticket

There are two types of traffic tickets: minor and major. A minor citation includes parking violations and equipment failures like a nonworking headlight. Major violations (sometimes called moving violations) usually occur when the car is in motion and can carry heavier fines and sanctions against your driving record. You can get tickets for speeding, phone use when driving, or after an accident. If you receive a ticket from a police officer, you may be asked to sign it. This is not an admission of guilt but just stating you understand what you were accused of doing; it serves as a receipt for both parties.

Any ticket, major or minor, will have a fine involved. As a driver, you can choose to pay the fine within the allotted time or request a court date to appear and dispute the charge. Most states assign points for more serious violations. When used, this point system identifies and penalizes high-risk drivers. When you first receive your driver's license you have a zero-point balance, or a "clean driving record." For instance, in my state you receive zero points if your registration is not up to date. However, an expired or suspended license is twelve points. Speeding in my state will cost you from one to five points, depending on how far over the speed limit you are traveling. Each state determines how many points you can have before your license is suspended or taken away. Insurance companies can increase rates if you have points on your driving record. Your insurance company has access to your driving records and uses them to determine how much you pay to be insured. Make sure you pay any ticket on time to avoid late fees, possible suspension of your license, and most importantly, to learn from your mistake.

You Get in an Accident

Sometimes, even if you are doing everything right, accidents still happen. If you are involved in a minor accident and your car is still drivable, move out of the road, stop your car on the shoulder, and call the police. The other driver should do the same. This is when you will need your insurance information to exchange, as well as anything else the officer asks for. Do not make any comments about fault, and do not apologize to the other driver. Simply wait in your car for the police. If you can, take pictures of your car and the other car to document damage. Do not let an older, more experienced driver intimidate you or push you to accept fault. Go over the moments leading up to the accident in your mind as you await emergency help or the assistance of an adult you trust. Be honest and clear when they arrive and notify your insurance company when you get home.

If an accident is more serious, remain calm. Take a moment to check yourself for injuries before getting out of the car. Call 911, either from the car or after exiting it. Once authorities have been alerted, check on other drivers involved and get yourself out of the road, even if the car cannot be moved. Often passersby will stop to assist victims of serious accidents. If this happens, ask them to call a trusted adult to notify them of the situation.

You Encounter Road Rage

Aggressive driving and road rage are defined as deliberate, malicious, unsafe driving behaviors. That can look like another car following you very closely, speeding, or preventing you from changing lanes. When aggressive driving escalates, it becomes road rage. Some examples of road rage are purposely hitting a car, gesturing, or throwing things at drivers. Although it is tempting to react, do not use aggression to respond to aggression. Instead, focus on the road and avoid eye contact with aggressive drivers. If you feel targeted and unsafe, call 911 using a hands-free device. If you can't call hands-free, find a well-lit, populated place, like a store or hospital, to pull over and then call 911. If you are confronted, lock your doors, and remain in the car until help arrives or the other driver leaves. Never pull over and try to reason with an aggressive driver.

You Feel Road Rage

Driving can be frustrating, but it is never a reason to drive aggressively. Before hitting the road, anticipate slow traffic, bad drivers, and weather delays. Being mentally prepared for obstacles makes it easier to deal with them calmly if they happen. If you feel frustration turning to anger and aggression toward drivers, deescalate the situation immediately. First, move away from the stress point if you can. Signal and switch lanes to avoid slow drivers or take an alternate route to avoid traffic jams. If you are still angry, it is best to stop driving. Exit the roadway (not on the shoulder) and find a safe place to park your car for a few minutes. Sometimes even a change of scenery can help you calm down. Remember, these obstacles are not unique to you, they exist for everyone.

A Friend Asks You to Drive Their Car

Let's say you and a friend head out on a day trip to the beach. After a fun day, your friend asks you to drive their car home because they are too tired to drive. Is this allowed? Or smart or safe? The answer is yes to all three, but only if done correctly. It is legal for you to drive a car that doesn't belong to you if you have permission from the owner or person operating the car. In most cases, insurance covers a car rather than a particular driver, so if a car has insurance, it doesn't matter who is driving. Make sure to ask about insurance before taking the wheel. Before agreeing to drive, check your own mental state. It is okay to say no if you are also feeling tired or concerned about your ability to drive their car. Or, offer a compromise where you split driving. If you decide to drive, take a few minutes to familiarize yourself with the car. Find the turn signals and windshield wipers. Adjust the seat so you can comfortably operate the pedals and move the mirrors as well. Before setting off, glance at the dashboard for any lights or warnings, check the fuel level, and find the speedometer. Then, take it slow and steady until you get the feel of how the car maneuvers on the road. Hopefully, your friend will be grateful for your help and will be the perfect copilot, helping with navigation, music, and other ways to make your job as driver easier.

Highway Tips and Etiquette

Chapter 1 covered some general rules of the road, but highway driving deserves its own section. Driving on the highway can be complicated, because it involves high speeds and multiple lanes of traffic. There are unwritten rules and etiquette for driving on the highway that help keep people safe among a high volume of cars that are all traveling fast. Below are some examples of highway rules that you may encounter. It is important to note that not all these apply to every highway trip but represent things you will find over time as you gain experience as a driver.

On and Off Ramps

Entering and exiting the highway involves timing and merging with other vehicles. The series of entrance and exit ramps from a highway is called an interchange. On an entrance ramp, turn on your signal, then check your blind spot for cars. Once you can't see any cars next to you in your side mirror, ease into the driving lane and slowly accelerate. It is important to get to the minimum speed limit as soon as possible to accommodate those already traveling at full speed on the highway. When exiting a highway, turn on your signal, then check your blind spot for cars before moving onto the ramp and decreasing speed. Note that those exiting the highway and entering it are often doing so very close together. Stay alert!

Passing

When attempting to pass a car on the highway, turn on your signal, then check your mirrors and your blind spot. When cars in that lane aren't visible in your side mirror, ease into the desired lane, maintain your speed, and deactivate your turn signal. Pass cars only when it is essential to maintain minimum speed limits. Frequent lane changes increase the chance of accidents. If a driver behind you repeatedly flashes their headlights, it means they want you to move over. This is usually due to slow speed. Simply move over when safe to do so and let them pass. Remember, on a multilane highway, you can pass a car in any lane. However, passing in the left-most lane requires that you move back over to your lane after passing, when it is safe. That left lane is not a travel lane like the right and middle lanes. One last note: Never use the shoulder or merge lane to pass.

Merging

Merges occur when you enter and exit roads. They can also happen when you lose a travel lane or enter work zones. Other cars currently on the road have the right-of-way when you are entering that road. If you are traveling a road and lanes merge, it is safest to alternate with other drivers to blend into one lane. Many people do not do this because they want to get ahead, or feel they have the right-of-way. Just make sure you are merging safely and using the every-other-car approach, and watch out for those not doing so. If someone is not letting you merge into their lane, simply let them pass, keep your signal on, and the next car should let you merge.

Large Trucks

After many years of driving, I still get intimidated by large trucks! Driving near trucks is easier if you relax and give them the space they require. Large trucks present unique challenges on the road. Their weight and size make it harder for them to stop. They also create large blind spots, called no-zones, requiring extra time and attention to pass them. It is best to not drive next to a truck; either go ahead or fall back so you always remain visible in a truck's mirrors. If changing lanes, wait until the truck is visible in your rearview mirror before moving into its lane to prevent a sudden deceleration. Remember that these drivers are usually trained but need a little help from the rest of us.

Speeding

It is easy to speed on the highway, as many people see the speed limit as a suggestion and not a rule. As a new driver, you know better and should model safe driving. Make sure to look for speed limit signs. Even highways have frequent changes to maximum speeds due to work zones, winding road conditions, or an area with many exits and entrances. Disregard people offering unsubstantiated advice like "You get a ticket only if you drive more than 10 mph over the speed limit." Follow the rules, and you don't have to do any calculations.

Tailgating

Tailgating refers to following the car in front of you too closely. Doing this gives you less time to react to sudden stops, causing accidents. Make sure that at least one car length is always between you and another car. In many states, if you hit a car from behind, it is automatically your fault regardless of circumstances. The law sees you as responsible for always maintaining a safe stopping distance. If you find yourself tailgating another car, slow down or pass the car. If you are being tailgated, do not speed up, but move over when safe to do so and let the car pass.

Tolls

Many highways charge a fee, or toll, for driving on that road. Sometimes tolls are optional, in the instance of express lanes on a highway where you can opt to take them or stay on the main road. Other tolls are located at the entrance to the highway and at each exit where you have to pay a fee. Many states are now using a pass system to pay tolls. Without a pass or device, your license plate is recorded automatically, and you receive a bill in the mail.

High-Occupancy Vehicle (HOV) Lanes

Many highways have high-occupancy vehicle (HOV) lanes or carpool lanes reserved for cars carrying more than one passenger. Typically, these lanes are used during specific times of heavy traffic, like morning and evening rush hour. They were created to encourage carpooling and help ease congestion. These lanes will be marked with black-and-white HOV signage. Be mindful of when HOV restrictions are enforced, as well as how many passengers are required (usually two or three). Outside of the restricted HOV hours, these lanes may be used by all cars. The fines for violating HOV restrictions can be more than $100. In some states, it can cost you points on your license as well.

Rumble Strips

You may have noticed wavy, raised pavement markers on the high-way. The markers cause a rumble and vibration when the tires cross them. These "rumble strips" are a safety measure designed to alert you when you have drifted out of your lane and need to correct. They are also used to slow down motorists before a sharp decrease in speed limit. Or, they can be along the center line of a two-lane road to prevent crossing into oncoming traffic or before a stop sign.

Safe Travels

Congratulations on reaching the end of this book! That was a lot of information to take in, but don't feel like you need to memorize everything here. You can come back to this book whenever you need to as you continue your journey as a driver.

You are embarking on an exciting time in your life, but driving comes with great responsibility. As you've seen throughout these chapters, there are many rules and regulations of the road. It takes practice, focus, and care to be a good driver and a good citizen to fellow drivers.

The best driving tip I can give you is to follow your instincts. Combine everything you have read here with real-world experience, and you will develop your intuition for recognizing when something is not right. Drive within speed limits, maintain safe following dis-tances, care for your car, watch out for bad weather, and read up on your state laws. You are well on your way to becoming a smart and responsible driver.

There is no telling where the road will take you in the future, but I feel humbled by the opportunity to equip you with the tools to arrive there safely. Good luck on the road, and safe driving!

BEFORE YOU GET OUT OF THE CAR: A CHECKLIST

Being a responsible driver does not end when you reach your destination. Once you arrive and park, there are certain steps you need to take to secure the car and ensure it is ready when you, or someone else, needs to drive it next. Here are a few recommendations:

- ☐ Make sure the car is in park.

- ☐ Engage the emergency brake if parked on a hill.

- ☐ Make sure all the windows are closed.

- ☐ Turn off the defroster or air-conditioning, if on.

- ☐ Turn off the radio.

- ☐ Turn off the windshield wipers, if on.

- ☐ Turn off the ignition and remove the keys.

- ☐ Check for passengers, pets, and valuables.

- ☐ After exiting the car, lock all doors.

- ☐ Ensure car is parked inside lines or close to curbs.

Answer Key

1. b	**20.** d	**39.** d	**58.** c
2. a	**21.** d	**40.** d	**59.** b
3. a	**22.** b	**41.** d	**60.** a
4. a	**23.** c	**42.** a	**61.** b
5. d	**24.** c	**43.** c	**62.** b
6. d	**25.** d	**44.** a	**63.** c
7. d	**26.** c	**45.** b	**64.** b
8. d	**27.** d	**46.** d	**65.** c
9. b	**28.** d	**47.** b	**66.** b
10. c	**29.** a	**48.** a	**67.** b
11. b	**30.** a	**49.** d	**68.** b
12. c	**31.** d	**50.** c	**69.** a
13. c	**32.** b	**51.** b	**70.** b
14. b	**33.** d	**52.** d	**71.** b
15. d	**34.** d	**53.** d	**72.** b
16. d	**35.** a	**54.** d	**73.** a
17. b	**36.** b	**55.** c	**74.** b
18. b	**37.** a	**56.** b	**75.** a
19. c	**38.** b	**57.** c	

Index

Acknowledgments

Here, I endeavor to capture everyone that paved the way for this book. My kids, amazing humans and drivers, who inspired me to start writing about the process. Mark, I never thought having a car-obsessed husband would be a bonus, but your help writing this was invaluable. My friends, sister, mother, and in-laws who suffered through my constant response of "I have a deadline." My amazing editors, Annie Choi and Connie Santisteban, who made me sound brilliant. My Grown and Flown crew for publishing the essays that started the book rolling. And my Maryland Girls—just for being you.

About the Author

MAUREEN STILES is a freelance writer and editor with a focus on parenting topics and general humor. She has been quoted in the *New York Times* and the *Washington Post* about parenting strategies. Her writing is featured on TODAY *Parents*, in the book *Grown and Flown: How to Support Your Teen, Stay Close as a Family, and Raise Independent Adults*, as well as myriad websites and blogs. Her blog *Magnificence in the Mundane* captures the chaos and joys of everyday life. Maureen is a native of Washington, DC, where she resides with her husband and three sons.